A N

A Norfolkman in the Raj

The Royal Artillery
1920-1933

Alan W Roper

Published by Adur Services Ltd

CONTENTS

Part One
In the beginning. Early memories of two young artillery men.

Part Two
Background to the North West Frontier and Tribal Lands.

Part Three
Home on the range. Day to day living conditions.

Part Four
Official list of battles and expeditions with added notes.

Part Five
Battery History 1919-26 with biographies of some of the officers and men.

Acknowledgements

I would like to thank all the people who have assisted me in making this book possible.

My wife Delia
My eldest son Mark
My nieces Elizabeth and Katherine
John Shaw (Passmore)
Margaret Poynter (Robinson)
Alan Tucker
Sidney Mann
Edward Jewson
Royal Norfolk Regimental Museum, Norwich
"Firepower" The Royal Artillery Museum, Woolwich
Imperial War Museum, London

FORWARD

Gunner Walter Roper was a professional soldier and in 1920 he was posted to India. Amongst his personal possessions was his "Brownie" box camera. The Brownie camera was mass produced, simple and inexpensive, as popular then as the digital camera is today. Between the two World Wars', greater comradery existed between the ranks, and I understand occasionally he was permitted to use a "Leica" camera. During Walter's service in India, he amassed a collection of over three hundred 'photos.

When discussing the book with a friend, Sidney Mann, he informed me his father was also an avid collector. Lt Mann was posted to India slightly earlier in 1918, and served in a Gurka regiment.
Sidney kindly allowed me to use some of his 'photos which assisted in the flow of the picture story, eg the arrival of the troopship at Bombay Harbour etc.

Walter's observations on fighting in the Tribal Lands and Afghanistan were: "It is not possible to win a war here, due to the terrain being vast and inhospitable".

Alan Roper
Norwich 2009

If we have inadvertently used any other person's 'photos, please advise and we will post an acknowledgement in future issues.

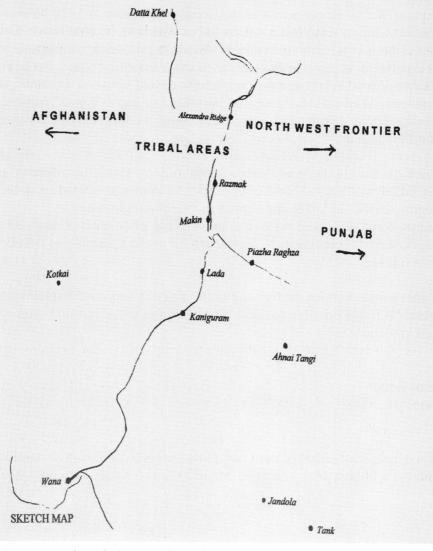

Distance approximately between Razmak and Wana 50 miles. The tribal Areas were administrated by political agents with British protection. The natives were not British subjects.

PART ONE

Early memories of two young artillery men

My father (Gunner) Walter Albert Roper was born in Southtown, Great Yarmouth on the 1st October 1896. His father Jonathan was employed as a stableman by Jewsons, who imported timber from Vyborg for local distribution. It could be said that Jonathan was Jewson's first transport manager. Walter had 13 brothers and sisters, births 1877 to 1903.

The children saw the holidaymakers as a much needed source of revenue. One of the smaller children used to fall off the end of the pier and after much wailing and screaming, an older child dived in to rescue the infant, meantime the other children passed round the hat! One of the pranks the children played on the local laundry was to wrap horse manure in towels and to leave the parcels with the other piles of laundry! Another source of amusement was the milkman, the children tied the wheels of his milk cart, they then roared with laughter at his look of bewilderment when he failed to progress. The boys' favourite sport was 'rat hunting' in the stables, care had to be taken to tie the bottom of their trousers.

Local women regularly made marked rounds of dough, the rounds were taken to the baker, who placed them on long wooden paddles, and slid them into a large oven. Half an hour later the heavenly smelling bread was collected by the families.

One of Walter's earliest occupations was assisting a local vicar with his small fishing craft. If the nets tangled, the vicar would bellow out the most vile obscenities. When Walter left school, his first full time job was working for a local shipbuilder, first assisting and then becoming a plate driller. Walter had no fear of the River Yare below, and much to the alarm of the other workers, he often pranced around precariously on the scaffolding.

In August 1914 young Walter (aged 17) decided he'd had enough of boring shipbuilding, he was seeking adventure in the war against the

Hun. Like many others, he lied about his age saying he was 18, he took the King's shilling and joined the Royal Artillery. The recruiting sergeants often turned a blind eye to the real age of a young recruit, as they received commission. In the Artillery Walter was employed as a Limber Gunner, his responsibility was for the gun's maintenance. The Limber was the undercarriage of the gun, which contained the ammunition and was attached to the two wheels.

Walter found France was not as exciting as he had envisaged. When asked about his great war experiences, he tended to be rather evasive. It was later revealed that in 1916 he was kicked by a horse and spent the final years of the war in and out of hospital. What he did recall was the revulsion of sometimes waking in the trenches and finding rats had been using his body heat for warmth! One incident he remembered was in the twilight feeling exhausted and looking for somewhere to sleep and in the grey mist he saw a partially damaged wall with soldiers asleep nearby. He was sharply awakened by the familiar whining and booming sounds of shells swiftly advancing towards the wall. He jumped to his feet and frantically shouted warnings to his slumbering comrades, without response. He shook the nearest soldier and suddenly realised he had been sleeping in a temporary cemetery!

1st July 1916 The Somme, France - in one day 19,000 men died and 57,000 injured.

"Some die shouting in gas or fire;
Some die silent, by shell and shot.
Some die desperate, caught on the wire;
Some die suddenly. This will not."   *Rudyard Kipling*

Armistice in November 1918.

Walter was a useful boxer and in 1919 he entered the Royal Artillery Boxing Championship at Lydd in Kent, he reached the final in his weight division. (See the photograph, he is the boxer facing the camera.)

On 6th May 1920 he embarked from Plymouth to India. Hopefully this adventure would be much more exciting than France. First the troops had to endure the Bay of Biscay, the mass of soldiers with sea sickness was unbelieveable. On 27th May 1920 he disembarked at Bombay, he was greeted with numerous welfare, church workers, etc, advising him of the dangers of India.

It made little sense then, but many years later his brother Arthur (who was a male nurse at Great Yarmouth Navel Hospital), was to tell him a very high percentage of hospital inmates suffered from venereal diseases.

At Bombay the soldiers were transferred to a transit camp, where they were fed and supplied with the remainder of their Indian equipment including a cork topee (helmet). They retained their 'Greatcoats'. Following the Crimean War every soldier was issued with a Greatcoat by a charitable trust. It was intensely hot and the new arrivals skins quickly turned to red. The shadows were deeply black and the sky appeared vast and blue. To the new arrival the atmosphere was both frightening and exciting. The days ended abruptly and overbearing heat could suddenly turn to freezing cold.

The Bombay railway station was an important commercial centre, crowded with beggars and vendors of food and drink, to some of the locals it was their home. The soldiers were issued with a basic packed meal prior to joining the train. The carriages had shutters which were kept closed during the hot season, there was no glass in the small windows of the "other ranks" carriages, glass would have increased the heat of the sun, and the outside air was allowed to circulate. The seats were bare strips of wood. The natives had to be removed from the sides of the train prior to departure. At various village stops poor quality food and hot tea was offered by the Army, or food could be purchased from the native vendors. The village stops had no platforms but the officers were able to leave their carriages by walking along the line and climbing up into the dining cars.

After a long exhausting journey, the train crossed the crocodile infested river Indus by the Attock Bridge, the gateway to the NWF. Several

11

other bridges crossed the River Indus, and approx a dozen ferries. The braver natives sometimes used inflated animal skins as boats. On the 3rd June 1920, Walter joined his unit: the 6th Pack Mountain Battery.

In 1888 Simon Passmore (the eldest son of Simon Passmore, Senior), was born in Devon, his father was a gamekeeper and Simon soon became a prolific rifle shot. It is imperative to restrict the number of wild rabbits, when their food is scarce, they then eat wood bark which kills the trees.

Simon's father was a drunkard. When returning home late at night he demanded a meal, which was inevitably followed by a beating for his wife. One day after his mother had received her habitual brutal assault, Simon gave the bully a vicious punch, knocking him out. He then decided it was time to leave home.

He joined the Royal Artillary, and at the commencement of the Great War, was promoted to Serjeant. On the 10th March 1915 in Givenchy, he was supervising a gun with the object of demolishing an enemy machine gun, when his men were subjected to heavy shelling and close range rifle fire, yet still they succeeded in destroying the hostile machine gun. For his gallantry Simon was awarded the 'Distinguished Conduct Medal'. In Exeter September 1915, he was to marry Mabel Marks.

Early in 1918 British troops were sent to Northern Russia to counter the large number of occupying German soldiers. The brief was successful in keeping the Germans pinned down in the region until the armistice.

In 1919 a Russian Relief Force was formed, the main objectives were the replacement of existing British troops and to assist the "White Russians" against the Bolsheviks in the Civil War. The British contingency included Simon Passmore. In May, Simon and his colleagues left Tilbury Docks for Russia. The British Army had initial successes against the Bolsheviks during which Simon was to be awarded the Russian "Croix St Georges". Elsewhere in the country the more revolutionary Bolsheviks were overcoming our White allies.

The British public saw no future in a further war against the new emerging Russian Red Army, so the wise decision was made to withdraw our troops. To Simon's delight our expeditionary forces returned home to Plymouth on the "Kilonan Castle". His family were there to greet him. His next assignment was to join the 6th Pack Mountain Battery on the North West Frontier, as Brigade Quarter Master Serjeant and married quarters were to be provided.

Prior to 1871 officers were able to purchase commissions. In the 1920's the majority of officers were descended from traditional Army families, many were born overseas and educated in England. The traditionists had served their country well, it was part of their breeding "to do the right thing", eg they knew a coward would be ostracized. Familarity breeds contempt etc. To the non-traditionists the "club atmosphere" could be daunting.

The "other ranks" consisted of older men who had fought in France, and new young raw recruits who had joined the Army due to the economic depression. Many of our allies had returned to their homelands after the Great War, they had little interest in British Imperialism. An exception was "Yank" Gunner Michael Lacey from New Jersey who was later to receive the Military Medal for bravery in 1920. The Indian Army still retained a segment of Irishmen who were offered their release following Irish Independence in 1922. Few appreciated returning home unaided, and there was a mixed response. One of the later young recruits was Gunner Horace Robinson born 1905 in Bedfordshire. He later moved with his family to Norwich. Horace was a quiet man, he immediately formed a lifelong friendship with Norfolk born Walter.

Recruitment Parade Circa 1915

Lydd Kent 1919. The boxing final. Walter is facing the camera.

Bombay Harbour. The troop ships disembarking. For many soldiers this would be their first sighting of the Middle East.

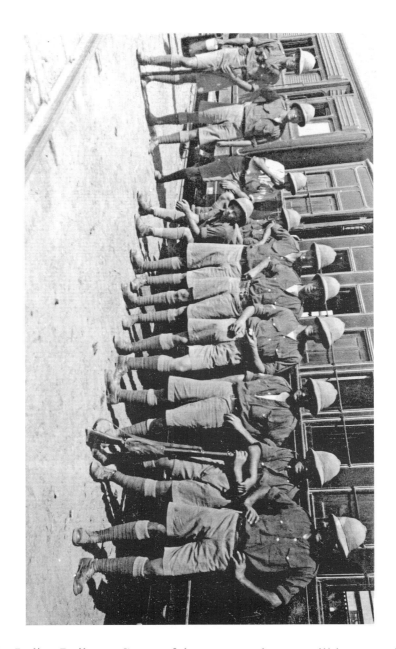

The Indian Railway. Some of the steam trains are still in use today.

The Attock Bridge. Gateway to the NWF and the Trible Lands.

Approaching the Attock Bridge

Simon Passmore

A Pontoon Bridge. Could be quickly assembled

PART TWO

Background to the Northwest Frontier and Tribal Lands

The North West Frontier lay between Afghanistan to the North and West, and the Punjab (Five Rivers) to the South East. The river Indus roughly divided the NWF from the Punjab. Afghanistan and the NWF borders were separated by the 'Durand Line; agreed by Mortimer Durand and the Afghan Amir in 1893. The 'Durand Line' was a loose double boundary which ran through the Tribal areas. The region was known to the British troops as "the grim". The area was bleak, grey and inhospitable. An arid, hilly, mountainous location with sharp plunging crevices, steep barren hillsides and abrupt ravines. The most fertile land was in the Vale of Peshawar.

In April until September the temperature could rise to 130F. The rains were not as fearsome as in central India. However it could be incredibly dangerous when the rain came cascading down the mountainside, in a deep, glistening, wall of water. The rainy seasons varied; one year might be continuous rain for 6/8 weeks, another year the rains could be intermittent. When the wet season abated it was followed by instant greenery; the croaking of frogs and the arrival of the harmless water snakes oozing through the black mud. When winter arrived it could become intensely cold.

The local crops were barley, apricots and sugar cane, mainly grown in the valleys. The animals were: fat-tailed sheep, camels, donkeys and buffalo, which were used for milk and the bullocks for transport.
The local tribesmen were Pathans, the Hindustani word for Pashto speaking people. Pashto was mainly a rich verbal language. The Pathan was a tall handsome muscular man, with shoulder length hair under a turban, a long loose often dirty tunic and baggy trousers and sandals. A cartridge belt was slung around his waist, he was accompanied by his inevitable jezail (a long musket). He would look you in the eye, and walk with an arrogant swagger.

There were estimated more than fifty tribes, each individual tribe is believed to have been descended from a single male ancestor, in turn each tribe was divided into clans, the Pathans were both savage and bloodthirsty, yet could be noble and hospitable to guests.

The Pathans terrorised the neighbouring regions like rampaging Vikings, stealing women, goods, animals, and kidnapping people for ransom. Their hostilities were necessitated because they were unable to sustain their families in their barren environment. Payments were made to responsible clans. Local Militia were recruited; allies were better than enemies.

The Imperial Army's main adversaries in the 1920's were the nomadic clans of the Wazirs and Mahsuds, particularly the Abdullai Mahsuds led by Musa Khan. Offending tribal villages were normally bombed or shelled. Families and animals were moved into the security of caves below the villages, which contained very vicious parasite insects. Reprisals against the nomads proved more difficult, as they vanished over the border into Afghanistan. Fortunately for the Imperial forces, there was a bitter land dispute between the two main tribes. Feuds were common between clans. Even villages had internal vendettas. Localised feuds were normally resolved within a short period.

Sir John Maffey, Chief Commissioner observed "In the passion for revenge, one murder leads to another." "In the case of murdered Europeans, if those who committed the crime are caught and hanged, the relatives will carry on what they imagine to be a blood feud, with Europeans as the object of the feud."

Within their own tribes, disputes were sometimes settled by Islamic Law, ie a woman who committed adultery, risked losing her nose through amputation. Likewise if a foreign soldier was captured, castration or decapitation was a possibility. In response the boys took few prisoners. During a melee, priority was given to the recovery of injured comrades.

"When you're wounded and left on Afghanistan's plains And the women come out to cut up what remains Jes roll up your rifle and blow out your brains An go to your Gawd like a soldier Go, go, go like a soldier"
R.K

In April 1919 an incident in Amritsar, Punjab, was to rock the credibility of the British in India. Mahatma Gandhi leader of the Indian Congress Party (who sought independence from Britain by peaceful means), was arrested. His crime was that he had ignored an order to remain in Bombay. There were protests. It must be remembered that many Indians had supported the British in the 1st World War against the Germans.

In the areas around Amritsar, the telegraph wires were cut, railway lines damaged, and a train derailed. On 13 April 1919 General Dyer ordered verbal proclamations to be made around the city. In the afternoon a large crowd of protestors gathered listening to a Congress speaker. In Dyer's opinion he had already issued riot warnings, so he ordered his detachment of troops to open fire, killing nearly 400 people. From Dyer's viewpoint it was a successful operation, others might disagree.

Afghanistan was ruled by a monarchy, similar to Shakespeare's "Macbeth", who thought little of murder, blackmail, etc to gain an advantage. In 1919 the Amir was killed in suspicious circumstances whilst out hunting. Two of his sons proclaimed themselves as the new Amir. The strongest was Amanullah Khan. Amanullah decided the time was ripe to lead a force against the British. The third Afghan war commenced on 6 May 1919.

The new Amir's timing was right. The Imperial Army was tired and demoralised following the 1914/18 1st World War. The army produced the splendid "field service pocket book", covering most eventualities. Unfortunately each adversary was different. Not all enemies were going to confront you like the Zulus or use the hit and run tactics of the Boars, or the trench warfare of the Germans. The most difficult opponents were proving to be the Afghans and the Pathans. When the columns were advancing along the valleys, bombs could be hurled from above. It was a snipers paradise. You cannot respond with heavy artillery or machine gun fire up the vast sheer terrain. The boys were not accustomed to the severe atmospheric conditions and ultimately the largest proportion of the columns consisted of Indian troops.

However the Amir had underestimated the depth of the Imperial Army's resources. Each side was to win various skirmishes but the deciding factors in ending the war was in May, the Amir's palace in Kabul was bombed by a Handley-Page aircraft, commanded by Captain Halley, and on June 1st, a relief force arrived, led by General Dyer. 8 August 1919 a peace treaty was signed in Rawalpindi.

Unfortunately the fleeing Afghan army had abandoned a vast amount of guns and equipment which the Pathans quickly retrieved. To the Pathan, a modern rifle was worth more than life itself. He could trade it for a piece of land and a harem.

The Indian Army consisted of various tribes. The Gurkas were first class troops. Their mountaineering background was advantageous in the Tribal Areas. The Sikhs were very reliable and brave. The Punjabi Mohomedan, the Dogras, the Jat and the Garhwalis and the Maharattas were fine trustworthy soldiers.

In late May 1919, 1000 + of the local (Wazirs/Mahsuds) militia mutinied taking their 303 rifles and ammunition. Initially the Mahsuds enjoyed success defeating Punjabi and Mahratta forces, killing over 100 men. The Mahsuds swordsmen were very effective at close quarters. Their marksmen were using smokeless ammunition and low-trajectory rifles.

Eventually the the Imperial Army overcame the Mahsuds with their firepower of long-range Howitzers, and shorter range Lewis machine guns and conventional long-barreled field guns.The original 7lb mountain gun was called the "bubble and squeak", this was superseded by the 10lb mountain gun. The 2.75 and 3.7 Howitzers were popular due to their weight, (the 2.75 weighed 10lb) and were easily assembled. The first Maxim machine gun was efficient but had a weight of 60lbs. This was replaced by the Vickers version with a weight of 34lbs, with a longer range than the Lewis. For firing bombs at high angles the Stokes mortar was a useful light short smooth bore gun, with a terrifying noisy florescent discharge.

The normal tactic was to take the high ground and build piquets (stockades made from stones, fortified with wire). When the piquets were used at night, nearby bushes were removed, (to stop the sentries accidentally firing believing them to be Pathans.) and bale wire from the bundles of animal feed were placed around the piquets - if the Pathans attacked, the wire would rattle. Special care had to be taken when withdrawing. The rear of the column was vulnerable.

The mules could be difficult and unpredictable but the raw recruits under-estimated their capabilities, they were able to assent quite steep terrain. The camels could only rest when their loads were removed.

Communications were then by pigeon, klaxon horns, telephone cables, verey flares, heliographs and radio. Heliographs were very successful due to the very strong sun. Messages were sent in Morse code. Radio was in its infancy and only used by the RAF.

High command were very concerned regarding the partial success of the hostile Pathans. Their improved performance was due to more advanced weaponry and British trained troops. Lord Montagu of Beauleu (adviser on Mechanical Transport Services in India 1915-19), was to report from January 1919 to the end of 1921, over 6,000 officers and men have been killed or died of wounds or diseases. More than 5,000 were wounded and over 1,000 were missing. Montagu was in favour of additional roads.

Various solutions were discussed, including the use of mustard gas but this was rejected. In the Great War gas had the habit of blowing back on our troops. More air power. The Bristol fighters needed to fly at very high altitudes, when low flying the planes could be shot down by rifle fire. This received a mixed response. Increased road building for more motorised vehicles (Ford vans were then in use). This was concluded as the best way forward.

A Wazir Warrior with his Jezail, a long
Afghan musket (see cover)

Death of a colleague
Killed in action 1917

Gun Practice

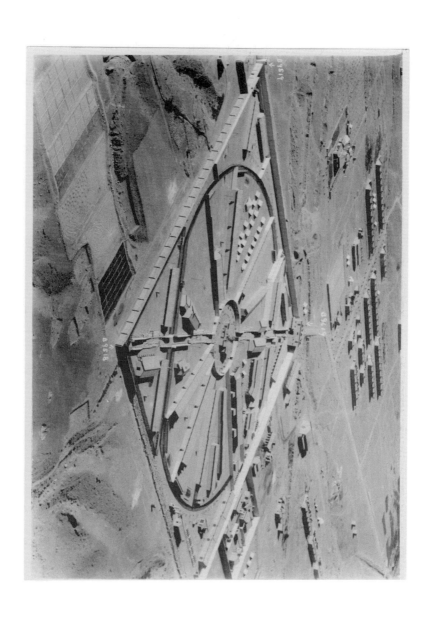

Typical Camp Layout

The Nomadic Wazir Tribesmen

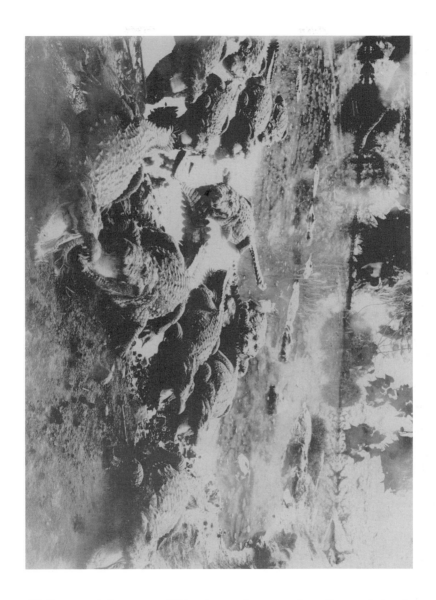

If dissected the crocodiles stomachs occasionally contained human remains.

Wild herds of buffalo grazing

Camels had to be unloaded before they could rest

Most Moslems would donate an Anna (a small coin)
when passing a beggar

Gurka troops. The Kukri (their well known curved knife). It was customary
when removed from the   scabbard, it had to draw blood. If not an adversary's
blood, the Gurka would nick his own thumb.

A native Jirga (meeting)

A fortune teller reading the beads

Camel Drovers

Snake charmer. Note the deep shadow of the watching soldier
in the foreground

Snake charmer
Would you like to meet him with his pets in the dark ?

A rural mosque.
Most Pathans had limited knowledge of the Koran and
relied on the mullah for his interpretation.

A former medieval stronghold, which had been converted into a fort

Dancing bears
Sadly their teeth and claws would have been extracted.

An overloaded buffalo
Buffalo were used for transport , meat and milk

Passing traffic - ancient and modern.

A Howitzer in action
They were capable of firing explosive shells or shrapnel and
possessed a greater range than the normal field gun

A Jirga (meeting).
A British officer explaining peace proposals. Note the two
rows of Indian soldiers. One inside the circle.

A railway ferry
Sometimes the rail gauges varied

A Piquet.
A stockade made from stone and wire. Normally topped with sand bags

A railway terminal - see the water towers and coal dumps

A mule loaded with Howitzer gun parts

A wheel and axle mule, loading by numbers.

Improved roads
The ford vans provided a superior and safer form of transport

PART THREE

Home on the range

The troops of the 6 Pack Battery regarded Razmak as their home. The large double camp was self contained and built on a high plateau. Being on high ground the atmosphere for most of the year was acceptable. The site was remote but accessible for trains and aircraft.

Ask any NWF veteran to reminisce about their memories of India, and their first recollection will be of the Kite (Shite) hawks diving down and stealing the raw recruit's dinner as they left the cookhouse, on their way to the dining areas. Red meat was normally leathery, due to the lack of fat and non aging. Walter's favourite meal was Irish stew. Additional food could be purchased from the camp wallahs. The wallahs (for a small payment) provided numerous services for the other ranks including washing and ironing their uniforms. The wallahs duties included cleaning the latrines. The faeces were deposited on tins, which were then removed by low caste wallahs. This practice still continues today in some country areas, for high caste Brahmins.

Life was generally conducted in a series of parades ie food, pay, inspections, and a Sunday church parade, plus one day of rest. The Army provided numerous sporting opportunities: soccer, tug of war, running, shooting, etc. The officers additional sporting activities included: polo and hunting, using imported hounds to hunt jackals, and occasionally point to point race meetings. Tennis was popular with the wives. The Indian regiments produced the best hockey teams.

Hunting in the 1920's provided a useful service. Jackals, crocodiles and tigers were all capable of carrying off small children. Tigers were known to take elderly native ladies working in the fields. The worst predators were snakes who killed hundreds of Indians every year. The camp dogs were fearful of the jackals who sometimes roamed the area. The white ants were a menace when in a temporary camp, they were liable to consume leather boots.

Walter's "D" Section of the 6 Pack Battery were very successful in winning the inter-battery sporting competitions. In 1923 they won the football, hockey and shooting shields. Simon Passmore was to win the Commanding Officer's Cup and Medal for best rifle shot in Battery.

The other ranks were allowed to keep pets. Dogs were the most popular. Other pets were monkeys, mongooses, parrots, etc. Baby bears were also kept but these had to be "put down" as they grew older. Care had to be taken with dogs as rabies was common.

The most popular entertainment was "housey housey" (bingo), followed by cards and Crown and Anchor. This game was played with a board, three dice and a cup. The board is divided into six sections: a heart, club, diamond, spade, crown and an anchor. Bets were placed on the sections. The dice are thrown. If a club, diamond and a crown were shown, each would be paid at evens. If one club and two diamonds were shown, the club would pay evens and the diamond two to one. Likewise if three anchors were shown, the anchor would pay three to one. It is obvious the advantage lay with the house. Walter owned a Crown and Anchor board, and was a very proficient card player, so he had no problem in subsidising his meagre Army pay. Officially gambling is prohibited in the Army but any NCO attempting to enforce this rule would have been naive.

Other entertainment was provided by native snake charmers, dancing troops, and dancing bears. The poor bears teeth and claws had been extracted. Sometimes the soldiers produced their own shows. The wallahs had a fear of the goat mascot believing him to be the British soldiers' God. Equally amusing was when the Pathans attacked an aerodrome, they fired into the roof believing that the aircraft were roosting.

The majority of troops enjoyed the route marches which normally proceeded at approx three miles an hour, with a short break each hour. The comradeship was marvellous. A struggling soldier would be assisted by his more active companions. In the first few days the soldiers feet would be badly blistered. The old army trick was to thread white cotton through the blister, which in theory soaks up the fluid.

Marching in reasonable weather conditions was a glorious way to enjoy the countryside. The column would pass the local transport, mainly consisting of noisy creaking bullock carts being coaxed and beaten by their impatient drovers. The band would play, and the men would sing their obscene versions of the songs. Nearing their journey's end they would sing "Polly Put The Kettle On".

The other ranks barracks were large with high ceilings. The kit boxes were used as private writing desks. Long tables were sited in the middle with benches. The beds were light with metal frames. Mosqueto nets were fitted at night. The cookhouse and latrines were some distance from the barracks. OR's had a strange habit of tucking their towels into the back of their shirts when they were washing, like sailors collars, probably because there were no towel rails.

Life was hard for the women in the married quarters. They regularly had to be prepared to pack at short notice, for transfer to a new camp. Because of temporary accommodations, flowers were normally grown in pots. All families had Indian servants, which did not suit all wives. Goods were purchased from the Army and Navy Stores catalogue. Payment was cash on delivery. Mabel and Simon Passmore were to have twins while in the NWF. A boy and a girl. The daughter was called Ladha (same as the camp) which she detested, and called herself Joyce.

In the Great War, Officers and OR's did not always enjoy a good rapport. Ordering troops from their trenches to their certain death was unpopular. Occasionally "it was believed a disliked Officer might die from "friendly fire". On the NWF there was a closer bond between ranks. However occasionally the lack of european women caused problems. A rumour circulated amongst the OR'S that a single Officer called A, was becoming too friendly with another Officer's attractive wife. Later when Officer B, was on manoeuvres he slipped and fell to his death in a bottomless defile. His body was never recovered. After the funeral B's "distraught" widow returned to the UK.

Statistically the ratio of deaths amongst officers was much higher than the OR's. The junior officers led from the front. A compensation was their holiday awards of six months in every two years. The OR's received two weeks each year, normally taken on their base camp or at a rest camp. Both Simon and Walter were devoted to the Army but Walter differed from Simon and rejected any offer of promotion. He was quite happy being a common gunner with no responsibilities. At times this could create problems ie if in action a member of the gun team froze, Walter would take their position.

His commanding officer Major Fowler, was to write in his annual appraisal "A very hard working, steady and reliable man, fit for a position of trust. Marked Excellent 1924. His appraisal had changed by 1926 to "No intention of rising above his present rank." Marked Excellent. His friends and colleagues were promoted including best friend "Robbo". The NCO's and the OR's were divided in their canteen by a rope. However, they still drank together by placing the tables adjacent to one another.

In 1926 Walter received a punishment. Apparently one of his friend's had produced a still, which made a type of hooch. The mixture was very potent, and the conspirators were soon highly intoxicated. Sadly one of his friend's was to die of alcoholic poisoning. The group were charged and convicted. The records were destroyed as usual two year's later.

April 1929 he became a member of the Royal Antediluvian "Order of Buffaloes". (This is a Masonic group within the Army), which is surprising as members were normally senior NCO's and above. October 1929 he became a Librarian, and later a storeman.

While in Razmak, Walter was delighted to meet members of the 2nd Battalion of the Norfolk Regiment. The Regiment was nicknamed "The Holy Boys" because they were said to have received a parcel of bibles from an elderly lady, prior to embarking abroad, which they promptly sold to buy beer! Walter's younger brother Arthur was also to join the Royal Artillery and follow him to the NWF.

Norfolkmen are normally perceived as being tall with blue eyes, a good physique and speaking with a slow, strong dialect. Known for their strange sense of oral humour eg "It's second on the right but if you miss the turning, it's first on the left when you return"! In 1933 he returned home. He was discharged having completed 21 year's service.

Razmak upper camp

Razmak lower camp

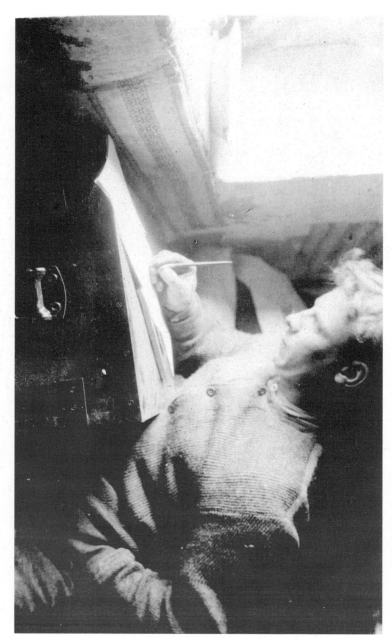

Dear mum, "I hope you are well"

"Get your feet off the bed". Reading was a popular past-time.

The weekly church parade.

The ORS barracks
Note the brick floors, and the racks for the mosquito nets.

Razmak Christmas 1928

Razmak Christmas 1928 (2)

Horace Robinson

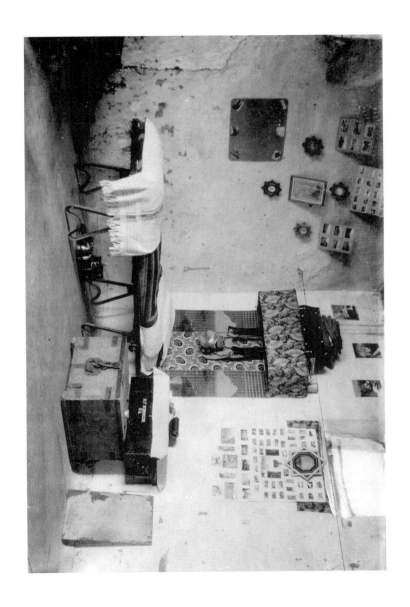

Horace Robinson's Corner - see his name on the box

The Dobie wallahs (washmen)
The wallahs washed, starched and ironed the soldiers uniforms.
The troops paid the wallahs a small amount each week directly for their services.

The boot wallah
All wallahs had to be first approved by the Senior NCO

"Your monkey Sahib"
ORS were normally allowed to keep one pet

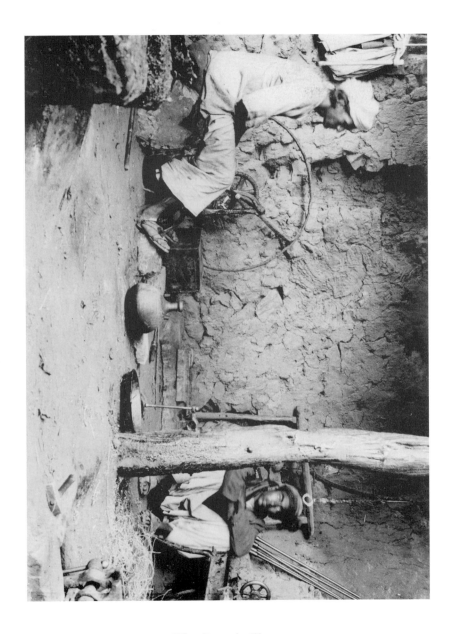

The Repair Shop

Mutton for dinner again!

The company mascot
Perceived by the natives as the soldiers god.

Royal Artillery Senior NCO's

"It ain't arf cold Mum"
The winters could become intensely cold.

Showtime
Whose turn is it to be the dame?

NCO's wife "The lady in white"
Can any reader identify her?

Razmak. The tug-of-war final

Fun in the snow

Walter's caption - "dodging stables again"
Walter is on the left.

A visiting native dance troup

Regular horse grooming was essential

Pigeon Post
Pigeons were still used for communications or kept as pets

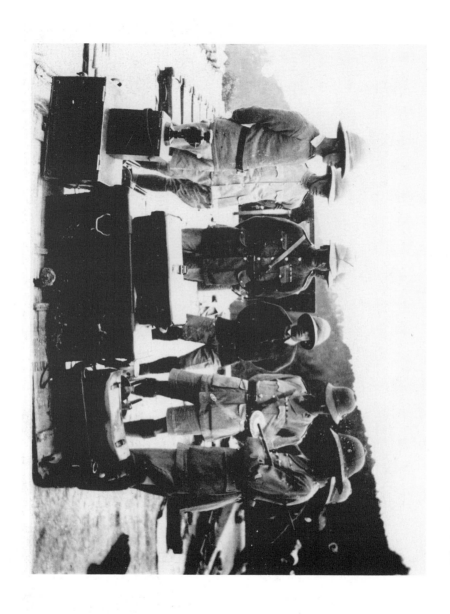

Senior Officers Inspection

Rawalpindi. On Patrol

Gun Park

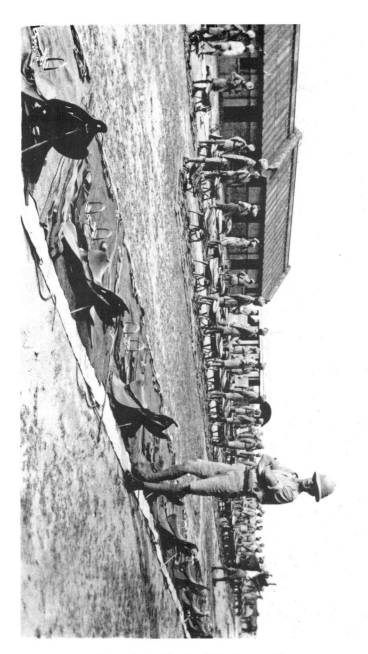

Rawalpindi - Saddle Inspection

Razmak a military train

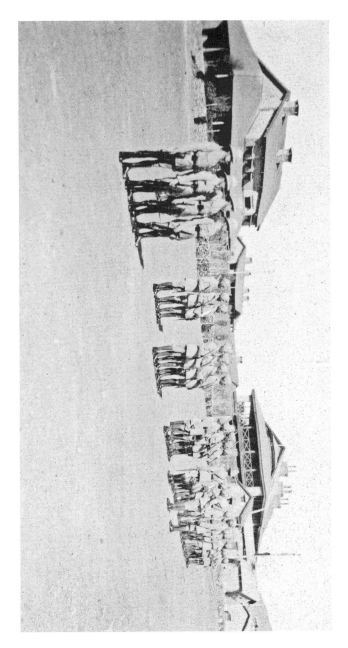

Razmak on Parade

A Jackal

Popular with the Officers when hunting, as a substitute for the fox.
Thought to be more cunning than the fox.   Feared by the camp dogs.

PART FOUR

LIST OF BATTLES AND EXPEDITIONS 1919-1926 KINDLY
SUPPLIED BY THE ROYAL ARTILLERY MUSEUM,
WOOLWICH

No 6 Pack Battery RGA
Transcript from Historical Records   (original transcripts and dates in
heavy type)
Mobilized at Peshawar and proceeded to the
Khyber with 1st Peshawar Division 05/05/19
PESHAWAR Important garrison town, Mohmand territory, fertile area.
KHYBER PASS A sparse, long winding pass. Very vulnerable to
attack from above. Historically used by many armies attempting to
conquer India, including Persians, Turks, Scythians, Mughals, Huns etc
Arrived Landi Kotal/Action at Bagh Springs 11/05/19
Afridi territory. Bagh = Garden
 Occupation of Datta Khel 16/05/19
DATTA KHEL, due to inexperienced junior officers, a large amount of
ammunition was wasted firing at shadows. DATTA Camp evacuated
Militia mutinied.
No 3 Section Afghan Boundary Commission 08/19
End of Third Afghan War.
Returned at Peshawar and proceeded to Waziristan 06/12/19
Action at Palosina 18/12-29/12/19
PALOSINA A Camp near Tank Zam (an artificial lake), heavy fighting.
Kot Kai 29/12/19-14/01/20
Army Camp. 50 Mahsud killed nearby.

Ahnai Tangi 14/01/20
AHNAI TANGI Camp at Ahnai. Tangi = gorge or pass. Very difficult
terrain. Column advanced too quickly, piquets had not been completed,
unnecessary loss of life. Lt Col Crowdy DSO Gurkha CO and his troop
ran out of ammunition. They then fought with bayonets. Crowdy was
killed

.

Sararogha 18/01/20-28/01/20 SORAROGHA An Army Camp on a plateau. Aerodrome site.

Piazha Raghza 06/02/20-15/02/20
PIAZHA RAZHZA Bushy area. The fanatic Mullah Lala Pir and Haji Abdur Razak were preaching rebellion to the local Pathans. The agitated Mahsuds then attacked the Imp Army 11 February 1920 A/Bdr G H Kilner RA, when under heavy fire he still maintained helio communications with the Artillery, directing their fire to a difficult target. Awarded the DCM, 2 February B/Q/M/S H Witney RA, his troops had evacuated their piquet. He remained issuing orders to the battery. His calm devotion to duty inspired his troops, who re-occupied the piquet. He was awarded the DCM.
Occupation of Makin 6/02/20
MAKIN A large Mahsud village, adjoining smaller villages. Makin was a tiered village built on the sides of hills. The more important buildings and towers were shelled and bombed. 25 February 1920 Lt Ernest B Pigott RA (6 Pack Batt) killed in action, awarded MC.

"A scrummage in a Border Station
A canter down some dark defile
Two thousand pounds of education
Drops to a ten-rupee jezail"
R.K

Kanigaram 06/03/20-08/04/20
KANIGURAM The Mahsud capital.
A ransom was paid to the Imperial forces.
Town not destroyed. Heavy snow.
Ladha 08/04/20-22/10/20
 LADHA Former main camp.
Jandola 24/10/20-11/11/20
JANDOLA Army Camp. Known to the troops as "the graveyard of the British".

Wana Column 11/11/20
WANA Secondary Imperial fort.
Occupation of Wana 21/12/20
Jandola 06/01/21-17/03/21
Ladha 19/03/21-11/12/21
10 April 1921 Sepoy Ishar Singh 28th Punjabis No 1 in Lewis Gun Section. He was severely wounded in the chest. His officers and NCO's were either killed or wounded, and his Lewis Gun was seized by their enemies. Singh located two of his colleagues and they re-captured his Lewis Gun. When his wounds were dressed he returned to assist in the recovery of his fallen colleagues. Ishar Singh was awarded the VC and later promoted to Captain. In late 1921 two 6" Howitzers were sent to Ladha. The towns of Makin and Kaniguram were within five miles of the fort, and in range of the new guns. In early 1922 it was decided that Razmak would become the main base because of its superior climate, and easy access.
Withdrawal of Wana Column 14/12/21-20/12/21
Rawalpindi 28/12/21-24/04/22
WANA April1922 F/O Chadwick-Brown pilot and observer F/O Jackson in their Bristol aircraft, were attacking hostile Wana Wazirs, when their plane developed engine trouble. They were forced to land. (see photo). Sqd Ldr Harris observing their difficulty dropped a message advising them to run to the nearby Wana Fort, approx two miles away. Meantime he circled overhead attempting to give them some protection. Their predicament was also observed by two other parties. Fortunately the local militia arrived first, two men with horses, followed by fifty or so hostile Wazirs, who succeeded in killing Jackson's horse. The small party escaped into the hills. Two day's later they arrived at Ladha Camp. The local militia were rewarded. Pilots were taught to speak basic Pashto for their own protection. They were able to say a "A large ransom would be paid if they returned intact". They also had this statement in writing:
Kalabagh, Hazara 28/04/22-08/10/22
Rest Camp
Rawalpindi 11/10/22-24/04/24

RAWALPINDI   Important Punjab city. Largest permanent garrison, and headquarter of northern command, with a rail link to Peshawar.
Bara Gali, Murree Hills 02/05/24-24/09/24
 Army Camp (see photo) A green fertile area.

Rawalpindi 28/09/24-25/04/25
Khyra Gali 28/04/25-28/10/25
Army Camp (see photo of native bazaar)
Rawalpindi 31/10/25-06/01/26
Akora 10/01/26-31/01/26
AKORA Annual Practice Camp. Co-ordination exercises between the RAF and the Royal Artillery.
Rawalpindi 04/02/26
Kalabagh (Hazara) 02/08/26
RAZMAK On a plateau and strategically placed between the Wazir and Mahsud's territories. The Razmak camp was divided into lower and higher camps, and at its maximum contained over 10,000 men. QUETTA Garrison town. 29 May 1935. The town was strangely still and quiet. 30 May a massive earthquake (measuring 7.7 on the Richter scale), commenced during the early hours lasting for approx six hours. The largest building, the town's prison, including inmates, plunged into the dark abyss below, leaving the remaining guards outside the prison in severe shock. The aerodrome was razed, with the deaths of 55 airmen and many more injured. Armageddon had arrived, and for six hours buildings crashed into huge crevasses. The loss of garrison, personnel and families was high. The total estimated number of people killed was in excess of 40,000. The remaining garrison personnel were evacuated to Peshawar.

AN INCIDENT OF INTEREST 2am on 14 April 1923 Kohat, Capt Hyland was sharing a bungalow with Major Ellis DSO. It was a stormy night. Doors and trees were banging and crashing. Hyland was awoken by the howling of his dogs. He proceeded into the other half of the bungalow where Mrs Ellis and her daughter had been sleeping. He was appalled to find the body of Mrs Ellis with her throat cut. 15 year old Molly Ellis was missing. Major Ellis was on duty. Hyland immediately gave the alarm, and search parties were quickly dispatched.

Many remember a similar outrage in Kohat in November 1920 when Colonel and Mrs Foulkes had been murdered. The Afridi tribe were obvious suspects. The kidnappers were thought to have gone to an area near Khanki Bazar. Reports were received that villagers near Kohat Pass had temporarily ceased a vicious internal war to assist in the hunt for Molly Ellis.

Even Kohat Pass Road, which was one of the main rifle trading areas, was quiet. Sir John Maffey, Chief Commissioner, speedily commenced negotiations with friendly Afridi tribesmen. After four days of exhausting travel by foot, Molly Ellis and her kidnappers arrived at their home in Tirah. The influential Mullah Mohammed Akhandzada was persuaded to assist. Molly Ellis was held at his residence.

Moghal Baz, Maffey's assistant and the lady doctor Mrs Starr, proceeded to the Mullahs home to negotiate Molly's return. Mrs Starr had previously experienced the horrors of the NWF. Both her and her husband were doctors at the Peshawar Mission Hospital. Late one night Dr Starr received a call to attend a sick person. Mrs Starr was to witness her husband's savage death on their verandah . The two women met in the Mullah's residence. Whilst they were talking, Mrs Ellis' killer Shahzada held Mrs Starr's arm and menacing threats were made, much to the disgust of the Mullah, as the women were in the sanctuary of his home. The outraged Mullah made arrangements for the ladies to be triumphantly returned.

Construction Work
The work was performed by native labour, supervised by Army Officers.

A native well

A young Hindu girl

Dera Ismail Khan
The River Indus

Officers 2/30 Pinjabs
Occasionally natives were promoted but never senior to a British Officer

Awaiting the command

A fallen comrade

Shahu Tangi (Tangi = a gorge)

Dargai Oba (Oba = water) 6th Pack Battery in action

Dargai Oba - 6th Pack Battery in action

Wana 1922
Flying Officer Chadwich Brown's plane developed engine trouble (see report)

Wana Fort

Inside Wana Fort

Taudachina (Taud = warm) (China = a spring)
Note the high observation towers.
The flat Roofs of the mud buildings were used as children' playgrounds.

Taudachina - Taking a short break

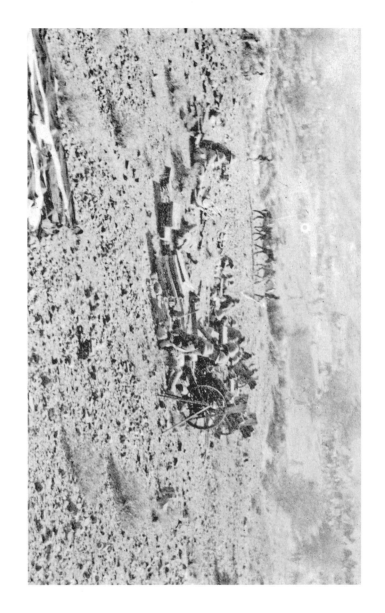

Dargai Oba - In action

A shelled village - retaliation for an earlier outrage.

A shelled hostile village.

Bibazai. Gun crew with their Gurkha allies.

Babizai Camp.

Bibizai - Time for a smoke.

Leaving a Masud village.
See the buildings on the brow of the hill

In Action.

Column climbing Spinshil hills. Spin = white.

A native regiment's bayonet inspection.

Tank Zam bridge Khirgi - On parade.

"We lost the wheel Sahib". Ford trucks were normally dependable.

Bristol aircraft normally flew at high altitudes.
A lone rifle could down a plane

127

A Bristol aircraft - The crew consisted of a pilot and an observer.

A town Mosque.

Rawalpindin railway station - Note the horse drawn taxis' (tongas).

Rawalpindi bazaar - most bazaars' were closed to other ranks

Khuyra Gali.

Khrai Gali - New acquaintances
See the two soldier s wearing caps. Photo shown before.

Khuyra Gali. - A few drinks later.

Khyra Gali - football champions 1924/25.

Khyra Gali. Bazaar

Attock fort.

A strategically placed fortress.

Murree hills NWF. -Note the abundance of pine trees.

Muree hills NWF - an attractive waterfall.

Murree hills - an ORS rest camp.

The troups could take their limited holidays here.

Quetta bazaar.
Quetta was the scene of the 1935 massive earthquake.
Measuring 7.7 on the Richter scale.

Peshawar city wall - The Indian army's northern headquarters.

Peshawar - a young leopard.

Peshawar Archaeological museum.

Peshawar - a tonga (taxi).

Alexandra Ridge fortress.

The Khyber Pass
A bullion convoy entering the pass, on route to the Amir.

The Khyber Pass. Known as the gateway to India.
Used by many conquering armies..
A long winding pass several miles across at its widest point.

Kojak Tunnel - the longest tunnel in India (three miles).

The Commissioner's house.

PART FIVE

Battery history 1919/26

On 3 August 1920, the designation of the Battery was changed from No 6 Mountain Battery RGA to No 6 Pack Battery RGA. On 24 May 1921 the Battery establishment changed to 5 British Officers, 1 Warrant Officer, 117 British Other Ranks, 2 Indian Officers, 172 Indian Other Ranks, 26 Followers, 16
Ponies MA and 163 Ordnance Mules.

In 1925 Major D Preston assumed command of the Battery. 13 October 1925 District Commander congratulated Battery on the very good condition of animals and good stable management. Battery won Artillery shooting cup for 4 years in succession: 1921/25.

GOC Inspection 17 April 1926 "An exceptionally smart efficient and well turned out Pack Battery with excellent spirit pervading all ranks" and very good unit - well officered - fit for active service." Major General Louise Vaughan, Commander Rawalpindi District.

30 October 1926 Major Preston, Lt Redman and 25 NCO's and men proceeded with Battery Records etc, to Egypt. 24 NCO's and men returned to the UK. Remaining 58 NCO's and men in India were posted to No 2 Pack Battery RA. Later designated 2nd Light Battery RA.

6 PACK BATTERY RGA ROLL OF OFFICERS WHO SERVED 1ST APRIL 1919-31 MARCH 1923 List of surnames kindly provided by The Royal Artillery Museum, Woolwich.

Major Edward Gardiner Fowler born 2 December 1879 died 19 March 1953 Gowran Castle, Kilkenney, Ireland. 2nd Lt 1899 Lt 1906 Major 1914 1919/21 Awarded CBE 1920/21 mentioned in Despatches.

Major Francis Ewan Mascall born 16 March 1881 overseas. 2nd Lt 1900 Lt 1901 Capt 1913 Major 1915. Later Lt Col. His father was a

Major in the Royal Engineers, who in 1885 became a Professor of Military Topography at Woolwich. Older brother of Brig Maurice Mascall. During the Great War Francis was awarded the Military Cross.

Major Gordon Steuart Low 1884/1956 Born Blackheath, Kent. A surveyor. Lived with his uncle a doctor, prior to joining the Army. 2nd Lt 1903 Lt 1906 Capt 1914 Major 1918 DSO 1919/21 mentioned in Despatches 1920/21

Capt Denys Oldfield Fardell born 27 September 1891 Hampshire Father Clergyman C of E. Mother was a Canadian. 2nd Lt 1912 Lt 1915 Capt 1916. Mentioned in Despatches 1920/21.

Capt Herbert Ernest Fooks born 14 January 1888 overseas. Awarded OBE. Married 1916 to Dorothy Fawcett.

Capt The Hon Dougall Meston born 17 December 1894 India. Died 2 January 1984. Educated Charterhouse - Royal Military Academy, Woolwich. 2nd Lt 1914 Lt 1915 Capt 1917. Retired from Army 1922. Became a Barrister in 1924. Contested the Southend by Election in 1927 as a Liberal. Runner-up to the Conservative candidate. Succeeded his father in 1943 as a Liberal Lord.

Capt Stewart Francis Montague born 12 June 1883 overseas. 2nd Lt 1902 Lt 1905. Officer i/c Gunpower factory 1910-1914 Capt 1914.

Capt Hugh Murray Johnstone McIntyre born 11 August 1892 overseas. Education United Services College, Windsor. Keen sportsman. A useful halfback. 2nd Lt 1912 Lt 1915, Capt 1916. Lt Col 1939.

Lt Eric M W Stevens born 24 May 1895 overseas. 2nd Lt 1915, Lt 1917, Major 1935, Lt Col Married Violet Grylls daughter of Major Grylls 1928.

Lt Stuart MacDonald Watson born 14 March 1898 overseas. 2nd Lt 1917, Lt 1918

Lt Gerald Tirah Palin born 20 March 1899 overseas. 2nd Lt 1918, Lt 1919. Acting Battery Commander prior to Major Preston's appointment in 1925.

Lt Ernest Borkman Pigott born in India, circ 1899 died 1920 of wounds in action. Sister Irene married to Capt Arthur Mathews, private doctor to the Viceroy Linlithgow and Earl Wavell. His cousin (who was a Forest Ranger) died with his wife when they were attacked by a tiger. Their only son aged 5 was orphaned.

Lt Francis Joseph Dillon born in Hendon on 19 October 1898 died 23 December 1975. The son of John Dillon, a company secretary to a public land organisation. His parents were born in England but their families had originated from Ireland. Living with the large family were his paternal grandmother, and their young domestic servant Blanche. At the age of 18 he joined the Army as 2nd Lt in the Royal Artillery. He was popular with all ranks and was nicknamed "Andy" by his fellow officers. MC 1919/21 mentioned in Despatches 1920/21. OBE, 2nd World War Brigader. Transferred to Singapore a few days before it fell to the Japanese. While escaping to Ceylon was unluckily captured by the enemy and returned to Changi. Sent to work on the Burma-Siam "Death Railway". Known for his bravery and decency. He fearlessly defended his mens rights. Half of his company were to die of illness and starvation in slave labour. After the war he became a business man.

Lt E C Miller   mentioned in Despatches 1920/21

2nd Lt Leonard Thomas Tulley born 1895 Southend, Essex. Died 1970, Father William a Consultant Marine Engineer.

2nd Lt T Gaskell   mentioned in Despatches. Afghanistan 1919

BQM Sgt Simon Passmore 1888 When Simon retired from the Army, he became a publican at "The George" in Cross Street, Colyton, Devon.

Other Ranks

BSM. W P Casey   mentioned in Despatches 1920/21

BSM. G G Price   mentioned in Despatches 1920/21

A/BSM. H Witney   awarded DCM 1919/21

Sgt T E Reed   mentioned in Despatches 1920/21

Sgt J McNamara   mentioned in Despatches 1920/21

Sgt B W Pilforld   mentioned in Despatches 1920/21

Sgt G W Kyle   awarded DCM 1919/21

A/Sgt F Lansbury   mentioned in Despatches 1920/21

A/Bombr H J Bowles   awarded MM 1919/21

L/Bombr Horace Robinson   1905/1979 When leaving the Army joined the local Gas company. Became a maintenance foreman in the Distribution Department. For many years lived in the appropriately named Gas Hill in Norwich. In the early 1950's the Roper and the Robinson families were to meet for the first time.

L/Bombr G H Kilner   awarded BSM Afghanistan 1919 mentioned in Despatches 1920/21

Gnr M Lacey   awarded MM 1919/21

Gnr W Lawton   mentioned in Despatches Afghanistan 1919

Gnr Walter Albert Roper 1896/1983 served 12 years in India. Returned to the UK in 1933. 1934 married wife Nellie. 1935 discharged from Army. Low waged work was provided for him in

Daughter born in 1935, died in infancy. 1936 became a postman. 1937 joined the T/A Inns of Court. 1940 called up for 2nd World War. Became a cook in RAC, 8th Army, Italy, Egypt etc.1952, discharged after 38 years service. 1962 Walter was awarded the Imperial Service Medal for charity work. In the 1980's he applied for a flat, in a new British Legion residential development being built in Worthing, (I lived nearby). Both my parents were bitterly disappointed when they received an unsigned rejection. Strange decisions were then also being made by Worthing Council (see Martin Short's book "In the Brotherhood"). Of course many members of the British Legion work long hours of unpaid welfare work. Walter died in Lewisham 1983. At the commencement of the Falkland War his comments were: "It gets your adrenalin going!"

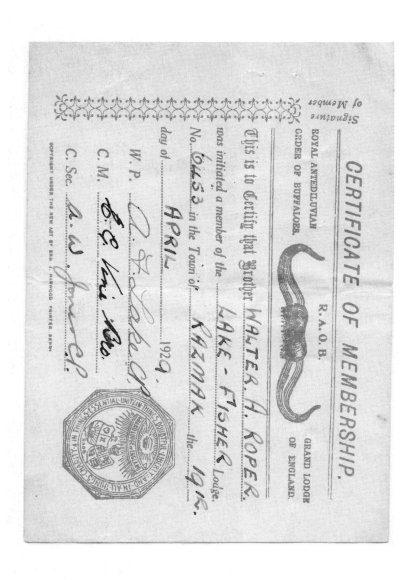

Certificate Of Membership.

A lodge meeting 1932
Walter is in the back row, seventh from the left.

The India general service medal 1908/35
The rear of the medal depicts the fortress at Jamrud in the Khyber Passs

Jamrud Fort.

Simon Passmore's medal
artillery match 1922

Simon Passmore's medal
"The "White" Russian Cross of St George. (We share the same Patron Saint as Russia)..

Simon Passmore's medal collection

The Roper Brothers 1914/18
Top left Robert (Army). Top Right Harry (Marines). Midd George
(Merchant Navy Capt) Bot.L John (Army). Bot R. Walter (Army).
George's ship is reputed to have sunk a U Boat by ramming.

The Roper Brothers in the 1960's
Left to Right Walter, John and Fred

Col. John Howlett Jewson 1895/1975

4th Batt Royal Norfolk Regt. Gallipoli and Palastine WW1. Received
The M/C at Gaza 1917. Also served in WW2.
When Chairman of Jewson's timber company, he awarded John Roper a watch
for 62 years service

The Author (centre).
Served his National Service in the R.A.F. Much to the disgust of
ex Army man Walter